# Introduction

It's 8.15 on yet another English Saturday night – the prattle of a football phone-in leaks from a stationary minicab, a dance anthem blares from an upstairs window and, across the street, the lights of the pub give out their usual muted welcome. Inside, the night is still young, although a predictable pattern has already settled over proceedings. Pale girls with impossibly thin arms sit around a low-slung table clutching drinks the colour of their dresses. An aging rocker plants his glass on the bar and wanders off in the direction of the jukebox. In a backroom, the evening's musical entertainer checks her make-up and adjusts her costume.

The images in Julie Henry's videos and photographs have a similarly haunting, even aching resonance. From amateur talent shows at workingmen's clubs to mod reunions in provincial dancehalls, from the seething terraces of football grounds to the brightly-lit video arcades at the Trocadero, Henry's camera highlights a series of beguilingly familiar scenes that are played out on a regular basis in towns and cities across the country but whose everyday pleasures and consolations are all-too-often overlooked. Sharply focused and unsentimental, Henry's work nonetheless possesses an almost nostalgic, bitter-sweet quality, as if aware of both the transience of these moments, and the increasing fragility of many of the working-class subcultures that sustain them. As pubs and clubs continue their makeover into gaudy sub-branches of corporate consumerdom, and as popular entertainment slips further under the spell of commerce and celebrity, Henry is not alone in finding solace in the spirit and camaraderie of older, more closely-knit communities. With visual adroitness, genuine pathos and obvious affection, her work celebrates the lives of what she terms 'local heroes' – the video-game whizkid, the pub sports hotshot, the talent show diva, the neighbourhood 'face'. Turning the spotlight onto people whose cultural activities and allegiances are rarely deemed worthy of wider exposure, she vividly reminds us that their talents and obsessions are, underneath it all, not so very different from those of the sporting icons and popular celebrities that mainstream culture chooses to elevate.

This is the first monographic survey of Julie Henry's work, and is published in association with Impressions Gallery, York, and Anthony Wilkinson Gallery in London. Showcasing five of the video and photographic pieces that Henry has produced over the last few years, it is designed to accompany a touring exhibition of her recent work, including a new Film and Video Umbrella commission, 'This Sporting Life'. My thanks go to all of the people who collaborated on this project (in particular Anthony Wilkinson, Anne McNeill, Paul Bayley and the staff at Impressions Gallery and Cornerhouse, Manchester). The fact that it has been such an enjoyable process for me and my colleagues at Film and Video Umbrella owes much to them, and not least to Julie Henry herself.

Steven Bode, Film and Video Umbrella

# Drawing in the Margins

As popular culture has become increasingly fractured and vari-form, the mainstream has become more and more tolerant of what once were considered 'subversive' activities. If, for instance, we were to follow the phenomenon of punk from its inception to its current position in society, we would trace a trajectory from dangerous antisocial behaviour to quaint curiosity to fashion conceit for ready consumption. Subcultures have developed into something other than the underground cabals of the post-war era. The music industry now looks beyond the populist majority to commercially viable micro-markets, while fashion houses take a more post-modern, pick-and-mix approach to garnering style references. This process of synthesising the marginal into the mainstream is often described as cultural homogenisation, but our personal perception of culture is more analogous to that of a view of a beach: from a distance, the illusion is of a single swathe of sand or pebbles; on a close-up, experiential level it is composed of millions of multi-hued aggregates.

Some theorists suggest that there is a mass culture imposed upon a powerless and passive people by a culture industry whose interests are in direct opposition to the people's, whereas others of a less cynical disposition argue that popular culture is progressive and essentially optimistic, with the vitality and motivation of participants making social change possible. This second model is the beach of possibilities where the subjects of Julie Henry's case studies pursue their personal ambitions. Henry's videos and photographs of people 'doing it for themselves' are studies of attempts to obtain if not broad social change, then at least self-empowerment. The work focuses on a range of leisure activities that, while not always exactly subcultural per se, lie somewhere between the evasion of and complicity with capitalist structures; entire worlds just below the parapet of commercial enterprise that ravel their own histories, identities and functions. Although many subcultures already subsumed by the mainstream are regurgitated as kitsch approximations of the original, Henry is interested in the authentic. By positioning herself not as a cynical observer, but as a sympathetic collector of documentary material, she gets close to the texture of real experience.

Henry's video 'Out of Time' (2001) documents the 'Outside Boots Brigade' from Cambridge. The membership is made up of men and women who, as teenagers in the 1960s, used to congregate on Saturdays outside their local branch of Boots. They now meet twice a year to dance to Northern Soul and celebrate their continuing existence. In a way, the gesture is one of aggrandisement, the mythologising of teenage banality. This extension of the ordinary into a time-honoured ritual asserts the importance of the brigade's collective past. In anthropological terms, this sort of temporal repetition is one of the more blatant forms of cultural evidence.

Henry herself grew up in Cambridge and, as a rite of passage, also started hanging out at the adolescents' hotspot a few years after the official core of the Brigade. Now an honorary member, she is eligible to attend their events, which she has filmed using concealed cameras. Unlike a plant in the audience that whips up a false reaction or a spy that pretends to be complicit, Henry's is a friendly presence. The video shows middle-aged men and women dancing to their signature Northern Soul track 'Out of Time', grinning, with their hands aloft. It is one of those lucid moments of joy that are usually helped along by the cloak of night and a veil of drink. By filming with miniature cameras hidden in hats, Henry not only avoids self-conscious performances from the dancers but also surrenders formal control over the final piece. Like an exercise in creative fatalism, the film engages a combination of determinism and free will: the cameras are orchestrated but the action is not entirely predictable, the fly on the wall is semi-authorial. The quality of the video, with its juddery camera movements and visible pixels that break down the image, contributes to the clandestine feel of the footage.

The history of Northern Soul itself lends another layer of cultural content. The musical genre came out of Detroit during the 1960s in the shadow of the Motown label, but without the same level of financial investment. Scores of predominantly black bands composed simple, optimistic songs in four-four time that just about anyone could dance to. During the 1970s, Northern Soul was picked up on in the north of England, according to some commentators, because of the region's affinity with mid-west American industrialism. The British appreciation of Northern Soul involved a more Baroque veneer, with athletic dancing incorporating talc-aided spins, leaps and acrobatics, all-nighters helped along with bananas and amphetamines, and an exaggerated reverence of DJs and their play lists. Even now DJs make trips to the mid-west to discover new 'big tunes' in thrift stores and return to a fanfare of expectation in the clubs.

Although Northern Soul has now been 'discovered' by mainstream clubs and radio DJs, the legendary all-nighters at Wigan Casino still have a place in popular mythology. Of course if everyone who claimed to have been there really was there, then Wigan pier would surely have collapsed under the weight. The Outside Boots Brigade's longstanding commitment, however, is apparent and, although their moves don't have the acrobatic precision of a Northern Soul impresario, the dancing has become a beloved symbol of their own geographical roots.

Accompanying the video is a panoramic photograph of the Brigade in front of Boots, with a key to the members' names. Although Henry's work deals with society in terms of cohesive tribes rather than conflicts between class or gender, it is interesting to note that only the men have nicknames: Dingle, Shilling, Ollie, Pinky, Dennis 'Up & Down' Doggett. The group portrait illustrates how a common geographic point encompasses a diversity of economic and social backgrounds, highlighting the truism that both individuals and societies are composite entities within which overlapping sets and subsets can delineate common ground or contradictions. The camaraderie of the Outside Boots Brigade comes not from a shared ideological or political position but from the arbitrary glue of nostalgia; the same nostalgia that has made the creators of friendsreunited.com a mint.

In her series of photographs, 'Talent Show' (2000), Henry pinpoints the tension between amateurism and ambition. 'Ordinary' people perform feats which, in the realm of television, are standard requirements but in reality are not so achievable by the majority of us. The professional entertainment industry lays a heavy burden of expectation on the amateur performer. In Henry's more pedestrian world, the singers, dancers, judges and audience establish an atmosphere that is deadly serious. The contestants train for months and are noticeably anxious at this final stage. Henry presents us with the moments that are mysteriously missing from the glossy world of film, theatre and television, yet she resists both the sentimentalism of 'Billy Elliot' or the sensation of 'Fame'. Her photographs are voyeuristic compared to, say, Powell and Pressberger's film 'The Red Shoes' in which, when not acting on the stage, the cast of the ballet are still acting on the screen, performing the performer. Henry, on the other hand, is interested in moments outside the consciously performative, eavesdropping on egos unaware of our secondary scrutiny.

The prevailing aesthetic of the contest is that parallel-style of cabaret: painted toenails, impossibly high heels, velveteen catsuits, shimmering silver backdrops and shot shirt cuffs. An overweight man with a 'Playboy' ring and suspiciously black hair is probably one of the judges. The venue is a universal every-place: a church hall with crucifix, clubhouse tables, plush-covered chairs and cheap, tubby wineglasses. The line between empathy and derision is very nearly crossed, as the tackiness makes us smile, but it is a smile that stops short of laughter. The role of the photograph has become that of neutral conduit so that the cynicism of the viewer is exercised while the role of the photographer recedes.

Whereas the documentary fact of the photographs elicits a judgmental response, the narrative of Henry's video work reframes subjects in a new context. The video portrait, 'X' (2001) shows the eponymous arcade game player as he achieves the highest score on the Star Wars game at London's Trocadero. In the guise of Luke Skywalker, he is engaged in one-to-one light sabre combat with Darth Vader – the highest level and ultimate goal of the game. We can hear the sound effects, see the astonished faces of two onlookers in the fifty-strong crowd in the background and the face of X himself as he squirms to the vicissitudes of battle. We see nothing of the battle itself. It is like de-centred porn, where the face in orgasm becomes the central image, a stand-in for the mechanics of coitus. Whereas in 'Talent Show', the individuals are very much aware of their own bodies and projected personalities in relation to the audience, X is absorbed by a fictional surrogate self with copious abilities – a sort of role-playing onanism.

The video game player can only act within the confines of preordained rules and game structures, so the minutiae of the programme must be mastered. X's technique is to turn off his light sabre until he knows that Darth Vader is about to attack, over-riding the ongoing depletion of his energy levels. Over many sessions, X has come to pre-empt the finite number of permutations within the programme itself and accordingly acts evasively or aggressively, proving that the artificial, finite intelligence of the machine is not necessarily supreme. X illustrates how imaginative manipulation can triumph over apparent immutability – 'local boy makes good', one of the classic folk narratives. 'X' is a humanist, almost spiritual proposition, suggesting that we can over-ride the restrictions of technology, as artificial intelligence is still inferior to the very human ability to learn.

At the moment of Darth Vader's death, as the familiar music swells appropriately, X allows himself a fleeting smile of victory over the leisure industry. But pathos lurks close by. We realise that although X is victorious, he is still pumping the machine and the capitalist structures that produce it with care-worn coins. He is paying for fantasy fulfilment, escapism and a temporary personality transference.

When opposing domination, we have two options: resistance or evasion. If, as suggested by the sociologist John Fiske, we take resistance to the dominant order as being the construction of new meanings, and its evasion the pursuit of uncommon pleasures, then by joining up the three points of the dominant order, evasion and resistance we can create a triangle of ideologies that represents regions of compliance, pleasure and meaning. Where might we place the activities of the naturist, the jaywalker or the hacker? They oscillate somewhere in the middle, moving towards or away from each apex as we consider them in different cultural or social contexts. Subcultures involve the interplay of meaning and pleasure, and Henry explores those that nuzzle fairly close to the dominant order. X and the Outside Boots Brigade neither wholly evade nor resist the hegemony of the leisure industry, but find a position that is subtly subversive yet ultimately complicit.

The status of the fan, from the hobbyist to rampant fanatic, occupies an equally indefinite territory. The fan of a band, film star, sports personality or team, by definition, wholly embraces the relevant industry. To purchase records, posters, scarves, t-shirts and tickets for games, gigs or films is to brand one's fidelity onto one's sleeve. However, this allegiance may be swapped for another at any time. The capriciousness of human nature is built into the very structure of pop and you will be nothing but encouraged to be inconstant. Unless it's football we're talking about.

The dynamics of football fandom – of the tribe, herd or mob, depending on your level of empathy with the game and its supporters – can be mapped in Henry's 'Going Down' (1998). Two monitors display opposing crowds of fans just as a goal is scored. The immediate impression is of a polarity of pantomime proportions, dictated by the direction of the advantage on the pitch. Cheers face howls of derision, punching the air counters swearing and gestures of outrage. Perhaps this performative behaviour is part of the role-playing element of being a football supporter, compounded by the presence of the camera. It is a rare instance of black and white in human affairs, a simplicity of division beyond most inter-personal relationships. Yet, like a microcosm of war, loyalties and power structures can be traced within each crowd. Individuals look to one another for affirmation while particular personalities lead subgroups. The whole is in a constant flux, an atomic reaction to the players out of sight on the pitch.

Although Henry is a life-long Liverpool fan, she spent a good part of the 1997/1998 season watching Crystal Palace. She got to know the regular characters in the crowds, learnt their songs and published booklets of their lyrics in all their expletive glory. These chants, like folklore, are passed on through an oral tradition, so by capturing their outrageous terrace wit in print, the song sheets become legitimate anthropological documents. The formal presentation of 'Going Down', however, propels it into something other than social documentary. The two video loops usher in a narrative element: caught in a football Groundhog Day, the opponents are destined to an eternity of exertion, sustained through Henry's manipulation of digital time. The f-ing and blinding man, the wild-eyed man in the hat and the bald headed man flicking Vs at the camera are like insects under glass, held forever as unfortunate specimens of fandom. This common view of the terrace as a seething primordial swamp, though, is not wholly accurate. Independent Supporters' Associations, or ISAs, have business as well as social functions.

The National Federation of Football Supporters' Clubs, founded in 1927, operated under the motto 'to help not hinder', providing financial support for clubs. In 1985, when the image of football was at a low ebb, with high-profile hooliganism and disasters such as the Bradford Stadium fire, the Football Supporters' Association was set up to organise fans so that their voices were heard and hopefully respected. Fanzines too, based on low-budget punk predecessors, have proliferated. It has been estimated that 600 football fanzines have been or are currently in circulation. Although many of the men in 'Going Down' seem unlikely ambassadors for the new responsible voice of football fans, they represent a far more cohesive rabble than they might first appear.

Another two-screen video installation, 'This Sporting Life' (2002), is Henry's most complex construction yet. The two monitors bracketed high on the wall tilt downwards as they do in pubs, directed towards the seated punter and out of the way of people's heads as they go to the bar. Archival footage from the 1970s pub sports series 'Indoor League' has been manipulated to resemble contemporary sports coverage. A table skittles match between old pro Dennis Jones and young upstart Philip Senior has been souped up with contemporary graphics, electronically remixed music commissioned from Andy Weatherall and three-dimensional computer reconstructions. Henry tracked down the original commentator, Dave Lanning, and asked him to contribute a new commentary for the additional computer-generated sequences so that the new package perfectly matches our experience of contemporary sports footage. It takes a while to realise that time has concertinaed, that the fashions clash with the slick rotating logos and the innocence of the original commentary sounds like an ironic pastiche of itself: 'Senior, the young man, the young man with the popstar hair.'

After the match, in which Senior beats the surreally respectable looking Jones, the winner is interviewed by star cricketer turned celebrity commentator, Fred Trueman. Awkward in his best clothes and nervous of the microphone, he is asked if he's ever played for £100 before. 'No, I think the last time I played for any money, it were two bob.' This is the sole voice in all of Henry's work. 'X', 'Out of Time', 'Talent Show' and 'Going Down' feature individuals as specimens of their type, but none actually reach us with their voice. What is striking about 'This Sporting Life' is how even though we can now put an accent, a vocabulary, and even a self-effacing personality to the individual, we still consider him a brew of archetypes. Proximity to a person should, like the close-up view of the beach, enable us to see the complexity of their make up but it seems that, through the dark glass of art, the camera lens or perhaps even the act of scrutiny itself, we simplify the chaotic to a more manageable resolution through a process of categorisation.

In the final chapters of 'War and Peace' Tolstoy indulges in a long and windy thesis on the nature of epistemology, society and history. Moving from grandiose meditations on the Napoleonic wars to a nuts and bolts ontological appraisal of existence, he acknowledges a very modern complexity. On the comprehension of cause and effect he states:

'Whatever presentation of the activity either of many men or of one man we may consider we always regard it as the product partly of freewill and partly of the law of necessity… The ratio of freedom to necessity decreases and increases according to the point of view from which the action is regarded; but their relation is always one of inverse proportions… A contemporary event seems indubitably the doing of all the men we know of concerned in it; but in the case of a more remote event we have had time to observe its inevitable consequences, which prevent our conceiving of anything else as possible. And the farther we go in our investigation of events the less arbitrary do they appear.'

The time span of a football or skittles match, talent contest or arcade game is such that, in retrospect, determinism appears to overshadow free will. The outcome seems to have been inescapable. But, by reducing these events to a fraction of their real running time, Henry re-inflates the element of self-determinism so that the central characters become autonomous heroes again. X, Philip Senior, Dennis 'Up & Down' Doggett and the singer in the velveteen catsuit are central points in their own mêlée of associations which can all be distilled into the fundamental dualisms of self and society, fate and freedom, the arbitrary and the ordered. Despite the deceptive simplicity of the work, it is a well-aimed lens that can assimilate these crucial complexities of leisure and pleasure.

Sally O'Reilly

# Going Down

For 'Going Down', I spent nine months at Crystal Palace football club. Unfortunately for them it was during their last season in the Premiership. The resulting video and photographs show the range of emotions experienced during the season. It was a dismal few months for the club and I found myself empathising with the supporters as I went through it with them. The video piece distils what I saw into a couple of minutes.

It contains the moment when the Eagles lose a goal to Coventry and both sets of fans' reactions. The Coventry fans chant 'Going down with the Villa'. It proves not to be the case for Villa, but is for Palace and the Palace fans respond with the customary defiance that had become their refuge during the season. This defiance eventually evaporates and is replaced with a rousing chorus of 'We're Shit and We Know We Are' towards the end.

I treated the photographs and the song sheets as a kind of hymn book. This was not my original intention but the most striking of the photographs contained quasi-religious poses that lent themselves to this.

I was fascinated by the huge potential for projection of emotions on to the players, the opposition fans and indeed on to each other. Spectators are able to experience hope, euphoria, sadness, loss, death and rebirth all in two hours on a Saturday afternoon.

This exists in other gatherings of people but this environment seems the preserve of masculinity, whatever your gender. It is a place where men can hug and kiss and it is socially acceptable.

Just don't try it in the pub afterwards.

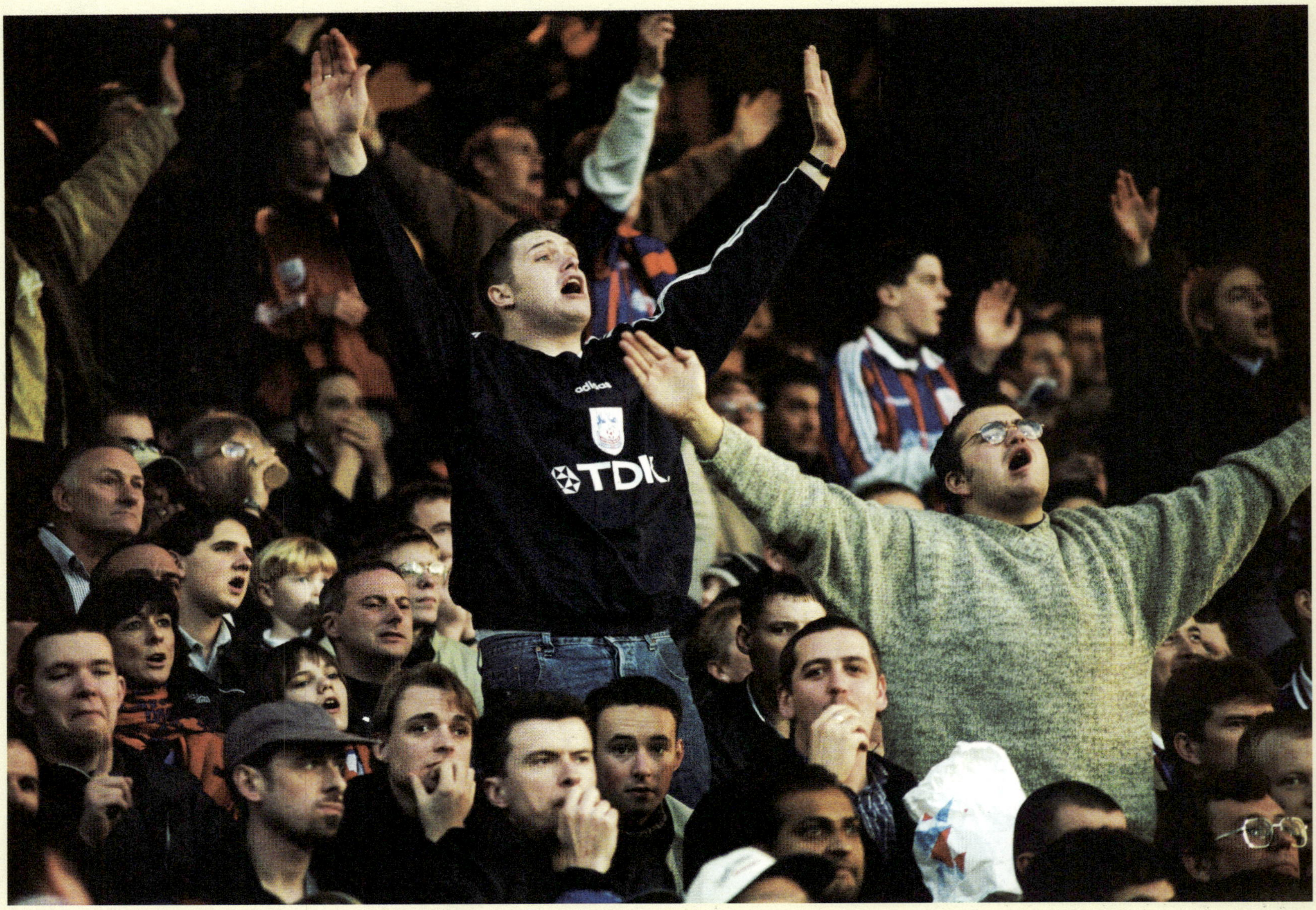


## The Great Escape

(Palace!)

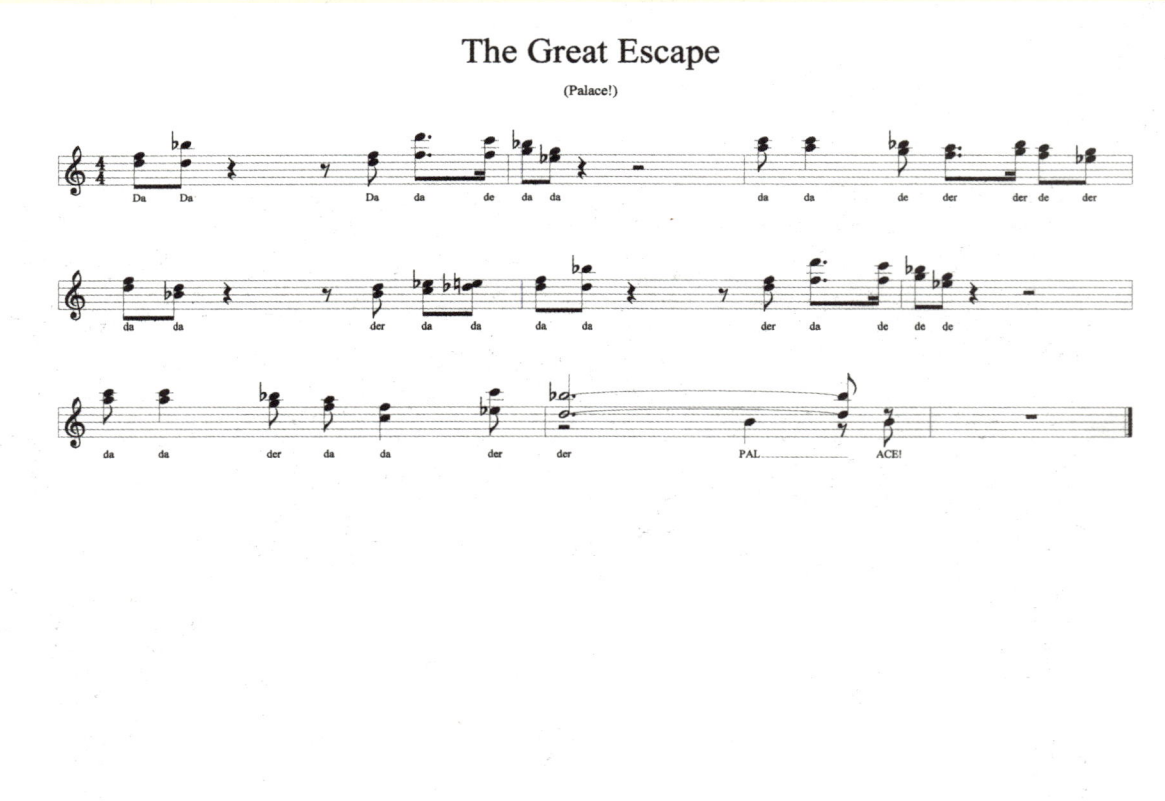

## You'll Never Walk Alone

We're in Therapy

I miss the first goal, probably as a result of the tea, but I hear and feel the roar. As I return from the toilet I come down the steps, above a sea of blue and white bobbing up and down deliriously. 'Down with the Villa, you're going down with the Villa'. Elation, aggression, dominance love and hate in equal measure.

Free Transfers

I look over their heads towards the Palace supporters away to my left. They are shouting abuse with distorted and pained faces. Their initial despair has turned to defiance, temporary defeat to a thirst for revenge. A small death and the hope of recovery. 'You've only got one song' is not the same class but it will do until the players on the pitch supply more ammunition.

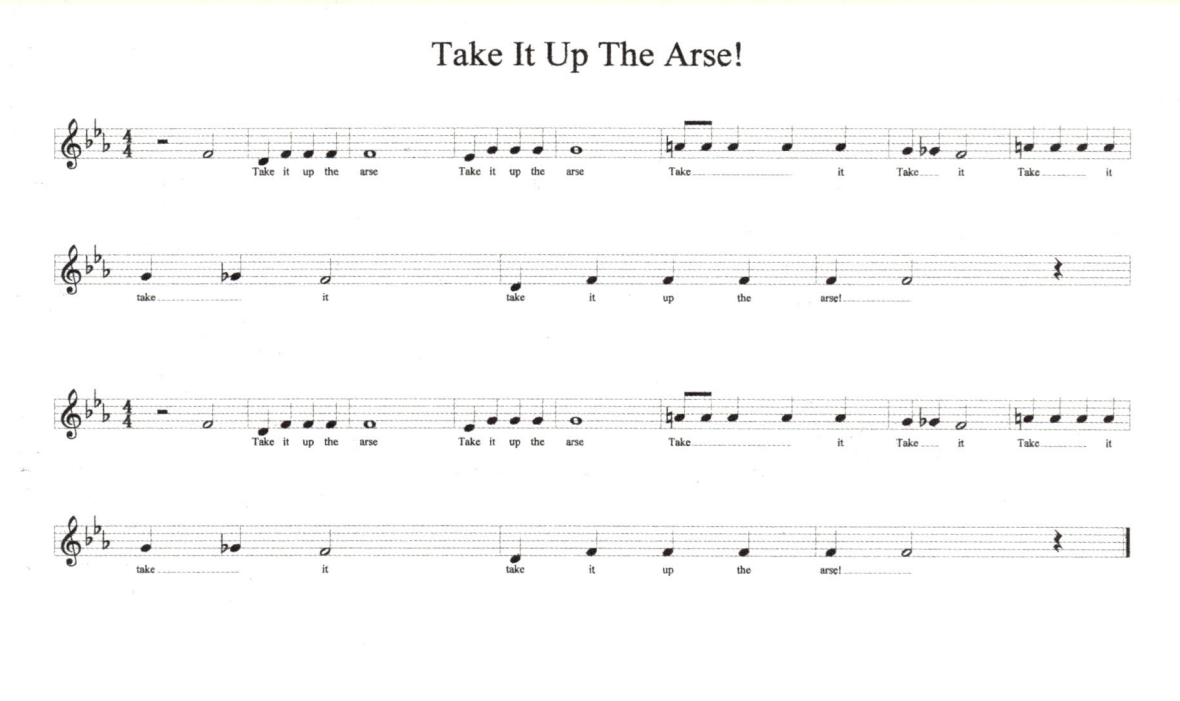

## Take It Up The Arse!

Take it up the arse Take it up the arse Take it Take it Take it
take it take it up the arse!
Take it up the arse Take it up the arse Take it Take it Take it
take it take it up the arse!

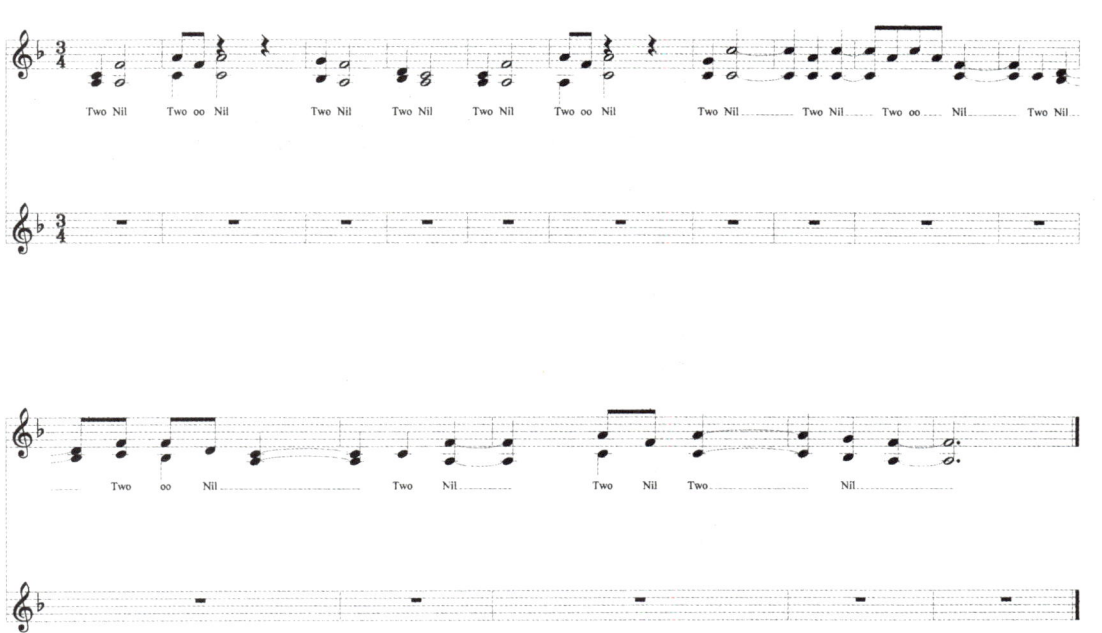

## Amazing Grace
(Two Nil)

# This Sporting Life

'This Sporting Life' looks at the still largely underground pub sports scene through the medium of a televised skittles final from the Seventies TV series 'Indoor League'. Pub sports (like skittles, bar billiards, darts etc) are still played regularly in many locals although they are becoming increasingly marginalised as pubs are revamped and refitted to appeal to a wider demographic. The graphics that I introduced into the video are designed to fit in with the period style of the original footage while mimicking the visual look and the hard-sell corporate branding of today's dedicated sports channels.

The winning finalist, Philip Senior, was not to go on to have a glittering career as British or world champion. Media attention and its associated rewards were denied him, but not because he was any less skilful than competitors in other sports. Our exposure to television sport, like TV's fascination with sporting heroes, has grown so much over the last thirty years that it is hard to remember how little airtime was once given over to now seemingly ubiquitous sports like football or snooker. Arguably, though, the 'innocence' and simplicity of that early coverage may actually be a closer reflection of the ideals and the spirit of sport than today's glitzy, round-the-clock TV spectacle.

By branding 'Indoor League' in the style of today's multi-channel TV environment, I am attempting to convey the drama and excitement of any sport in a language the contemporary viewer will understand. As a result 'This Sporting Life' has become something of a double-edged sword – part confirmation that you can sell anything if it is packaged well enough and part affirmation that you can't.

'Table skittles is one of the oldest pub games in the business.

It is very simple.

From 101, you get three throws and you must finish exactly on your number...'

'Now here's Dennis Jones

trailing... needing a big one...                    ...it's on, it's definitely on.'

'...Oh he's missed it
    HE'S MISSED IT COMPLETELY...'

'Watch for the round ball, the back two, the cross-shots, the outside two. These are the difficult shots. It's so important to get that first ball working for you and leave that follow-up throw...'

'...He can't find that fronter. Another lackadaisical shot...'

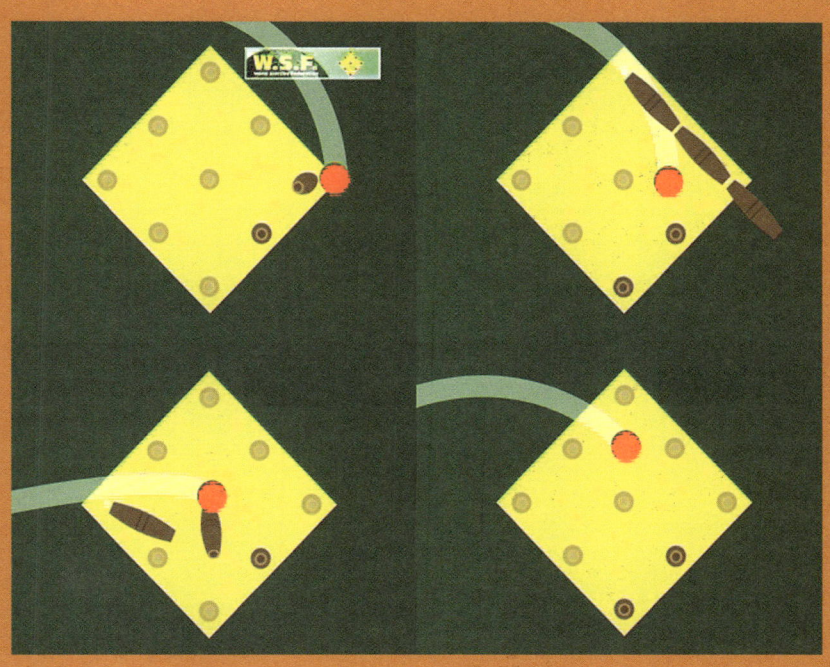

'It's a Flopper…'

THAT IS A FLOPPER…'

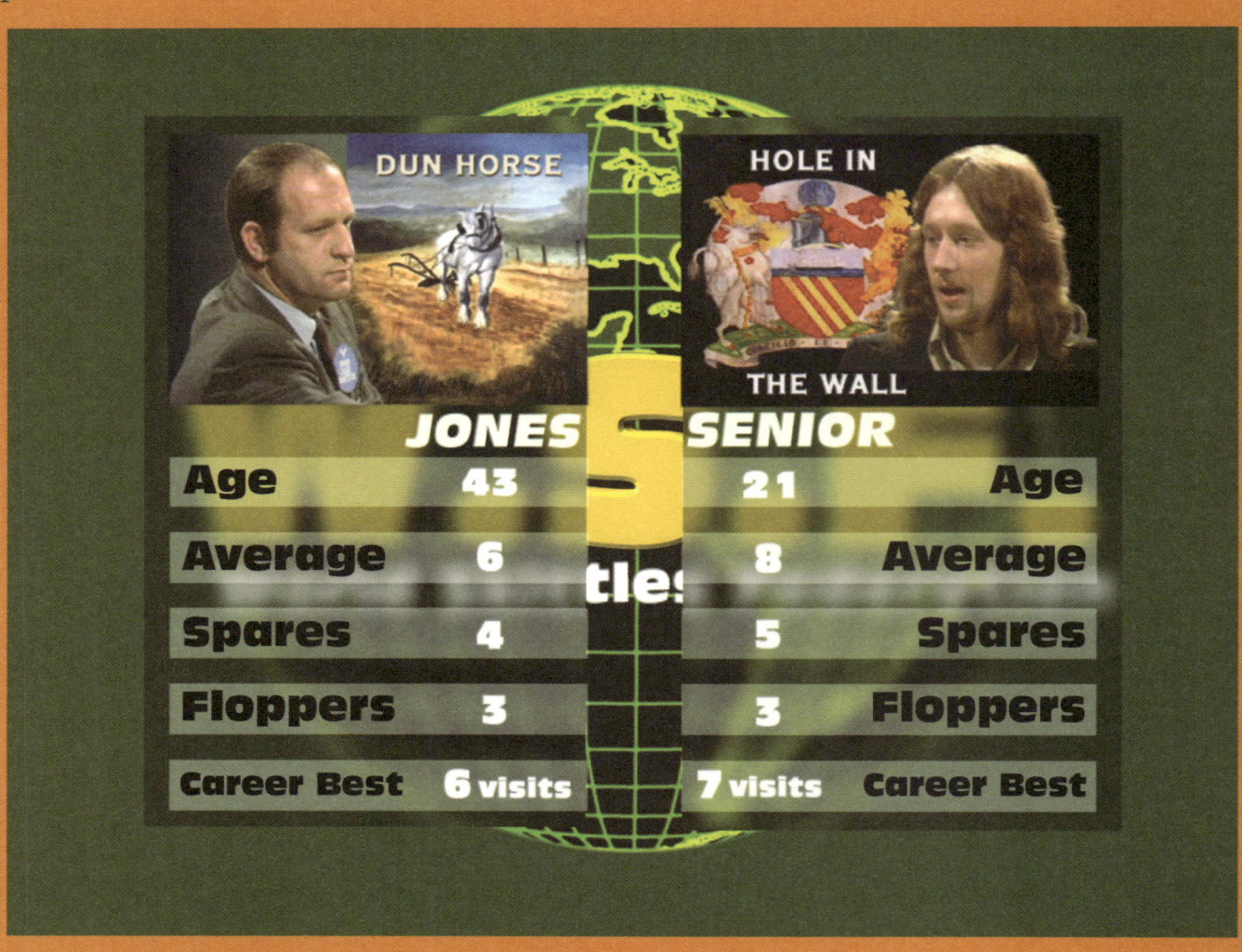

'…Master Senior made a mistake and was lucky to check out.'

'...Now let's hear him with Fred Trueman who's skittled a few in his time.'

Cornerhouse, Manchester

# Out of Time

The Outside Boots Brigade is a 'club' whose prerequisite for membership is having stood outside Boots the chemist in Cambridge as a teenager on Saturday afternoons in the mid to late Sixties. For 'Out of Time', I covertly filmed members at one of their regular parties. Two of us had cameras hidden in our hats, and three stills cameras were clamped to a gantry at the side of the venue. These were fired at random intervals throughout the evening. I had little control over the results. And in a way, I didn't want any. Instead, I wanted to capture some of the feeling of unpredictability that characterised my early dance club experiences.

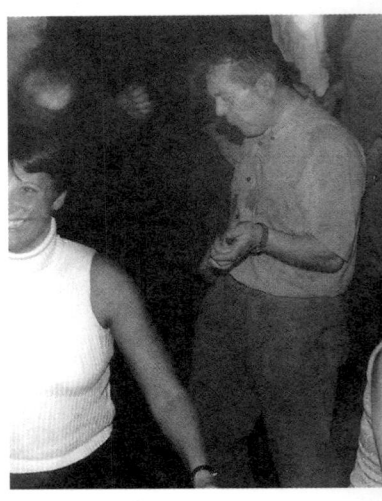

The resulting video piece shows a group of people dancing in a similar fashion to each other, to the song that has become their theme tune, 'Out of Time' by Chris Farlowe.

We see them raising their arms and clapping their hands in a style associated with religious worshippers, sports fans, political devotees and other groups prone to collective celebration and displays of solidarity.

They do this twice a year in affirmation of life and suspension of death.

They have done so for the past thirty years.

Cambridge, 1969

Cambridge, 1969

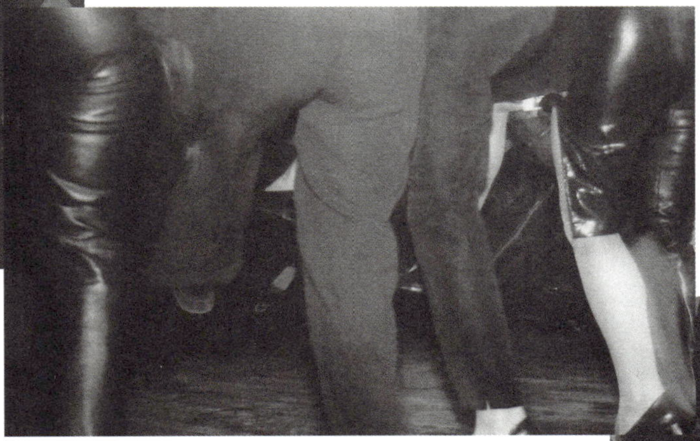

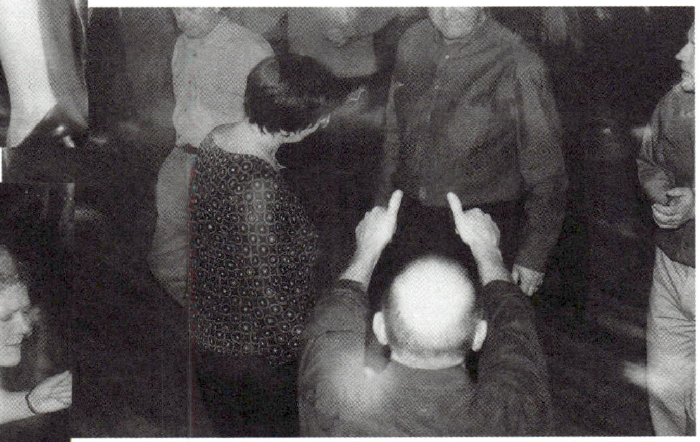

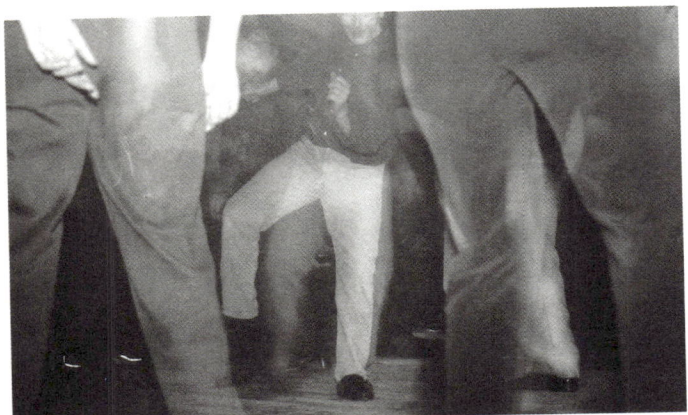

Impressions Gallery, York

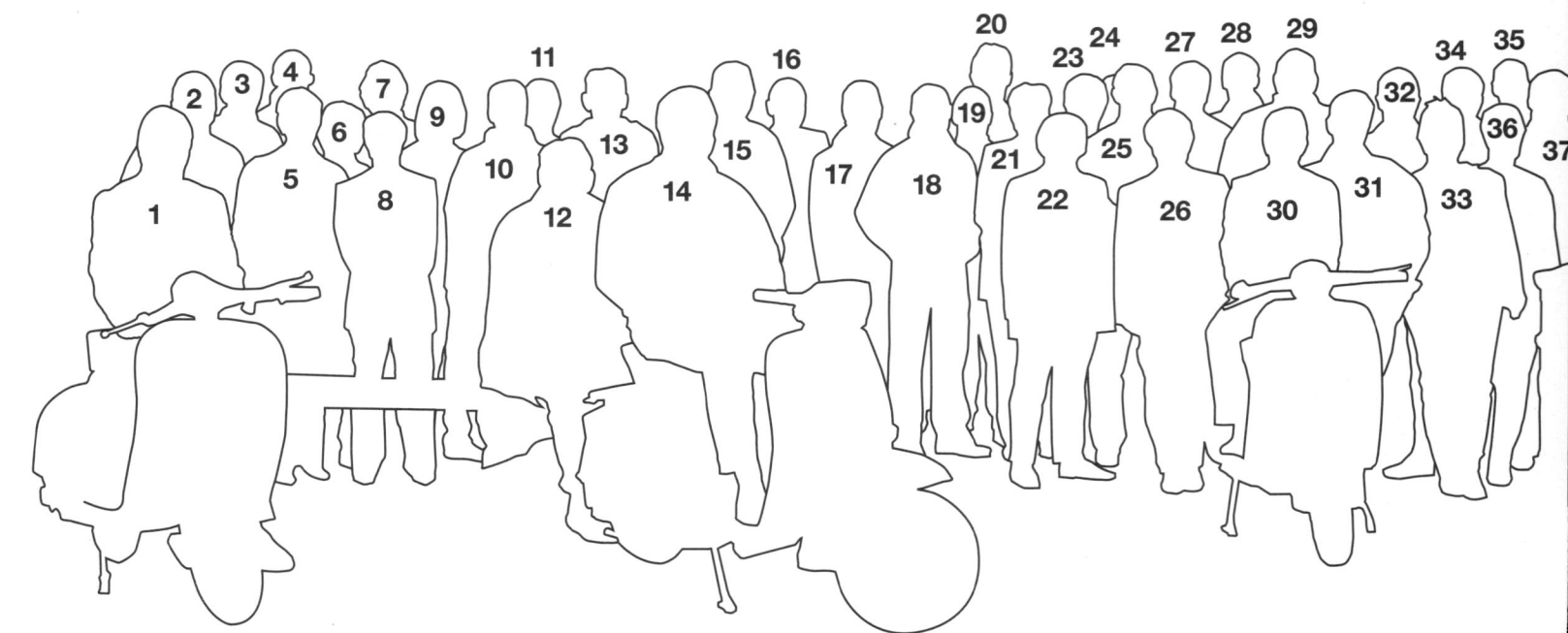

| | | |
|---|---|---|
| 1 Roger Gascoigne (Shilling) | 11 Libby Abbott | 21 Lisa Carlton |
| 2 Steve Stubbings | 12 Dave Garner (DJ) (Dingle) | 22 Wendy Pink |
| 3 Dave Addicott | 13 Terry Garner (DJ) | 23 Maureen Harding |
| 4 Colin Hopkins | 14 Malcolm Powley | 24 Penny Binge |
| 5 Cheryl Flitton | 15 Pat Clark | 25 Cliff Stamp |
| 6 Christine Hopkins | 16 Karl Conrad | 26 Mary Garner |
| 7 Kevin Newnham | 17 Anne Railton | 27 Ray Carlton |
| 8 Jill Flood | 18 John Railton (Johnny) | 28 Malcolm Binge |
| 9 Martha Powley | 19 Les Croucher | 29 Dave Pink (Pinky) |
| 10 Kim Browne | 20 Barry Harding | 30 Lynne Stubbings |

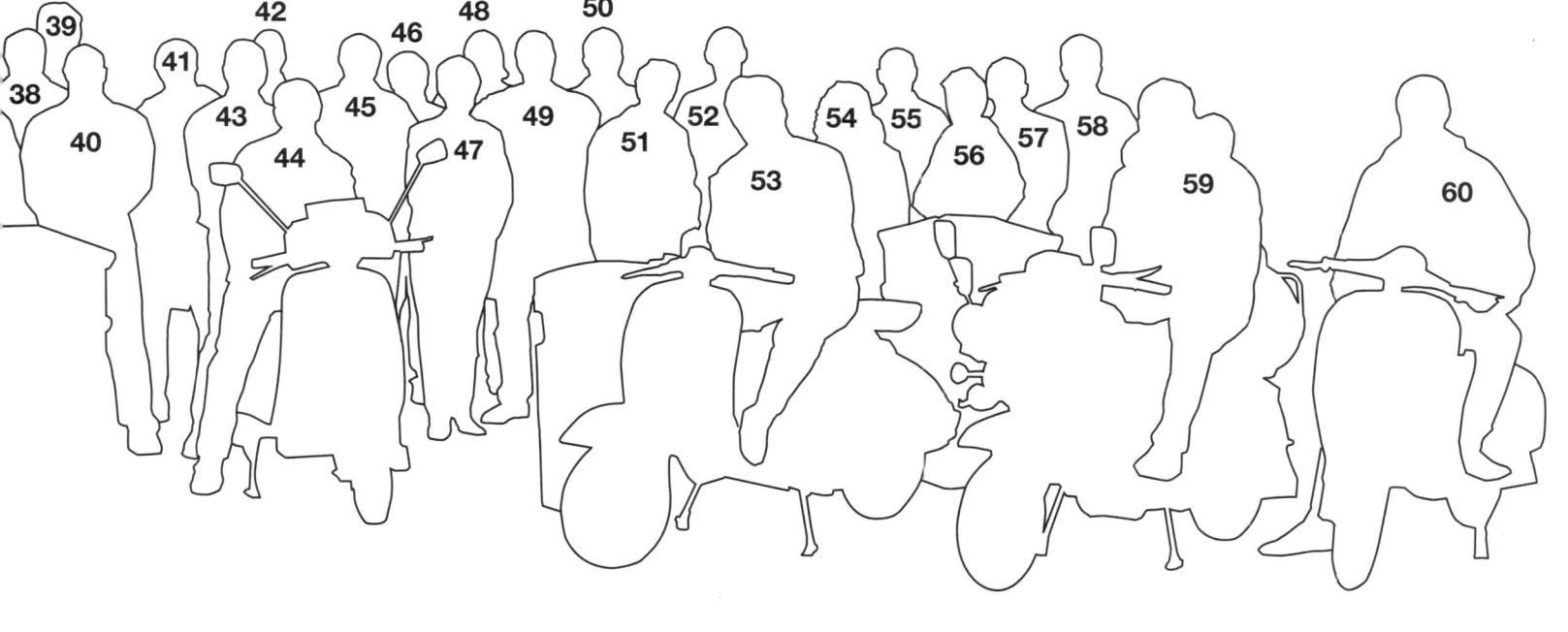

| | | |
|---|---|---|
| 31 Sally Claydon | 41 Robin Claydon | 51 Mick Peck |
| 32 Mick Potter | 42 Charlie Browne | 52 Gary Mader |
| 33 Dorothy Harman | 43 Colin Parsons | 53 John Abbott (JA) |
| 34 Angie Amps | 44 Colin Hall | 54 Jenny Mader |
| 35 Bob Amps | 45 Brian Wright | 55 Graham Flitton |
| 36 Jackie Elsom | 46 Terry Jones | 56 Sandra Charles |
| 37 Colin Davidson | 47 Linda Jones | 57 Oliver Digney (Ollie) |
| 38 Dennis (Up & Down) Doggett | 48 Ann Washbourne | 58 Graham Williams (Bill) |
| 39 Paul Belcher | 49 Bob Verrinder | 59 Simon Parr |
| 40 Kevin Wood | 50 Paul Washbourne | 60 Paul Sawtell |

# Talent Show

For this body of work, I attended and documented the heats and finals of two talent shows in the East End of London over a nine-month period. I spent time in the homes of contestants, interviewing them about their motivations for being involved in the shows.

I found a rich and appreciative culture that was outside the restraints of mainstream forms of entertainment. The shows are financed by the people who enter and attend, as well as by raffles, bar sales and refreshments. They exist not as a result of slick marketing and glitzy surroundings, but because the people involved support and sustain them.

I also found people who were dedicated to what they do with a single-mindedness that saw them talk of their career in the same breath as that of Frank Sinatra or Madonna. This could be seen as delusional but when you think about the cult of celebrity, the only thing that separates them from these people in real terms is exposure and money. I didn't find the performances any less entertaining.

If talent is based on the ability to deliver rather than the spending power of producers and entertainment companies, then what I was seeing was truly a talent show.

# X

X is the self-styled signature of a young games player. He has the highest score on over thirty machines in London's Trocadero. The piece shows him playing 'Star Wars Trilogy' on which he is capable of completing the entire game without missing a target. 'X' focuses on his face and the faces of two of the fifty-strong crowd behind him.

His relationship with the machine is one of total control. He has recreated the game in his own image, adding flourishes using features designed for functionality to further enhance his already impressive performance.

When he switches off his light sabre halfway through a duel with Darth Vader the gasp from those watching is audible. When he reignites just in time to execute a 360-degree sweep blocking his nemesis's next attack there is silence and knowing smiles. He is the best and everyone watching knows it. More importantly, he knows it himself. The smiles and gestures and the total confidence he exudes in each break in the game contrast sharply with the focus and concentration of the action sequences.

What separates X from thousands of other players in other arcades is the fact that he hits everything, he never misses, there is no let-down and scrambling for change before the continue counter hits zero.

Everyone participates in the hyper-reality of the situation. There is simple elation at having been there and having seen it happen. Our relationship with the pre-ordained commercial world is not always one of subjugation and this seems to me to be part of the watchers' thrill and fascination.

Impressions Gallery, York

'…You underestimate the power of the Dark Side…

…Obi-Wan has taught you well…'

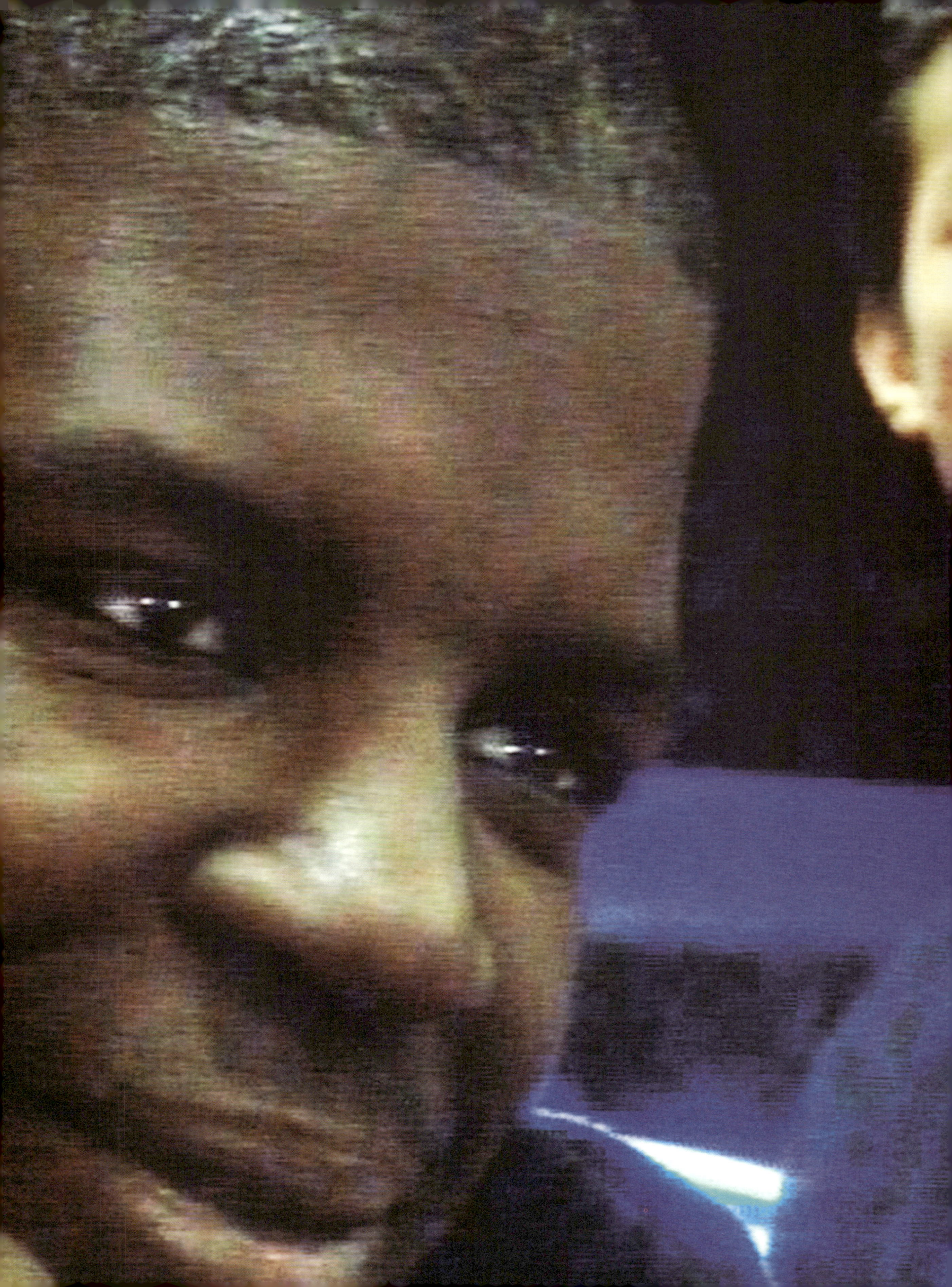

'…Impressive. Most impressive. But you're not a Jedi yet…'

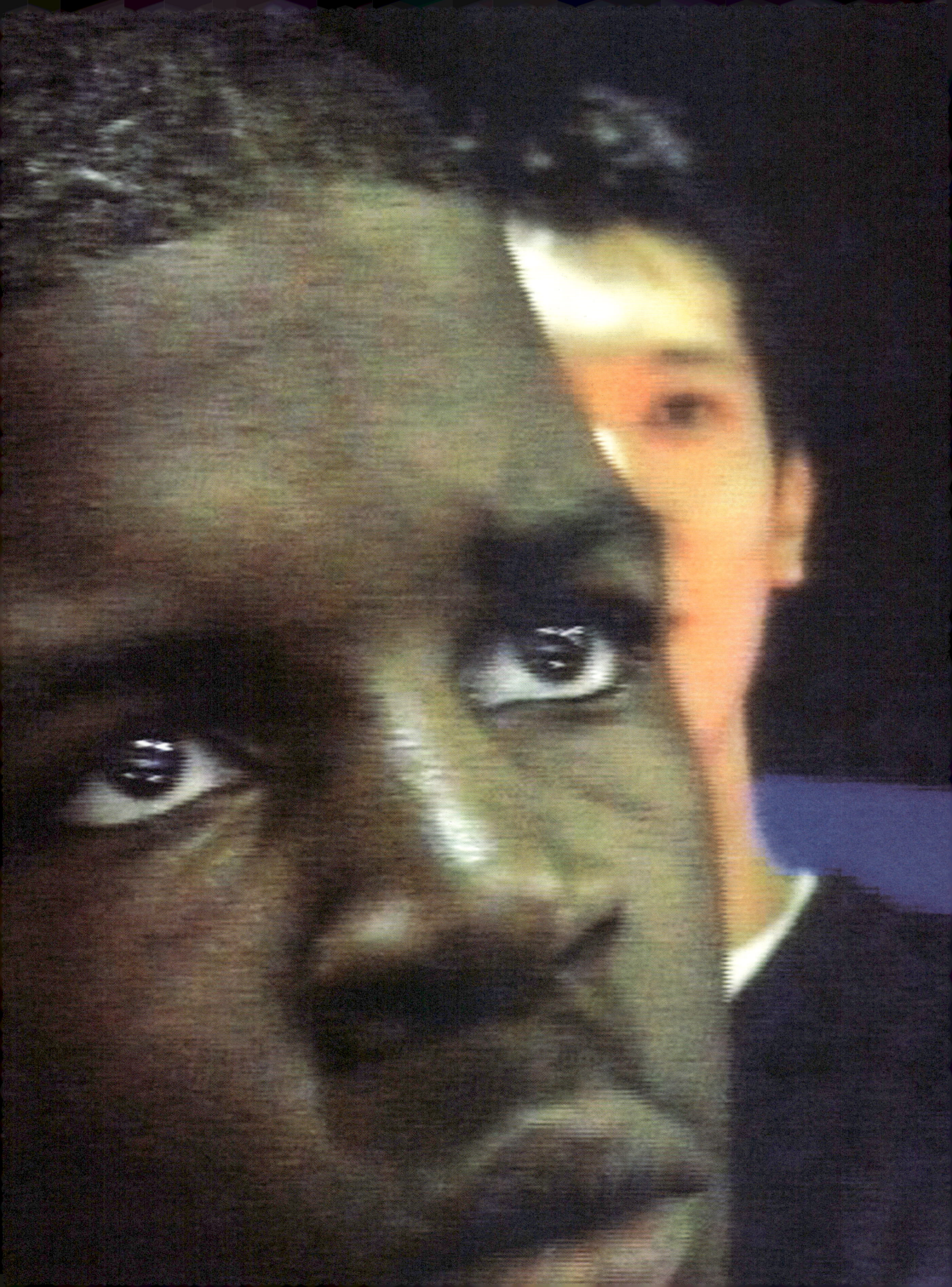

'...Your skills are complete. So be it, Jedi...'

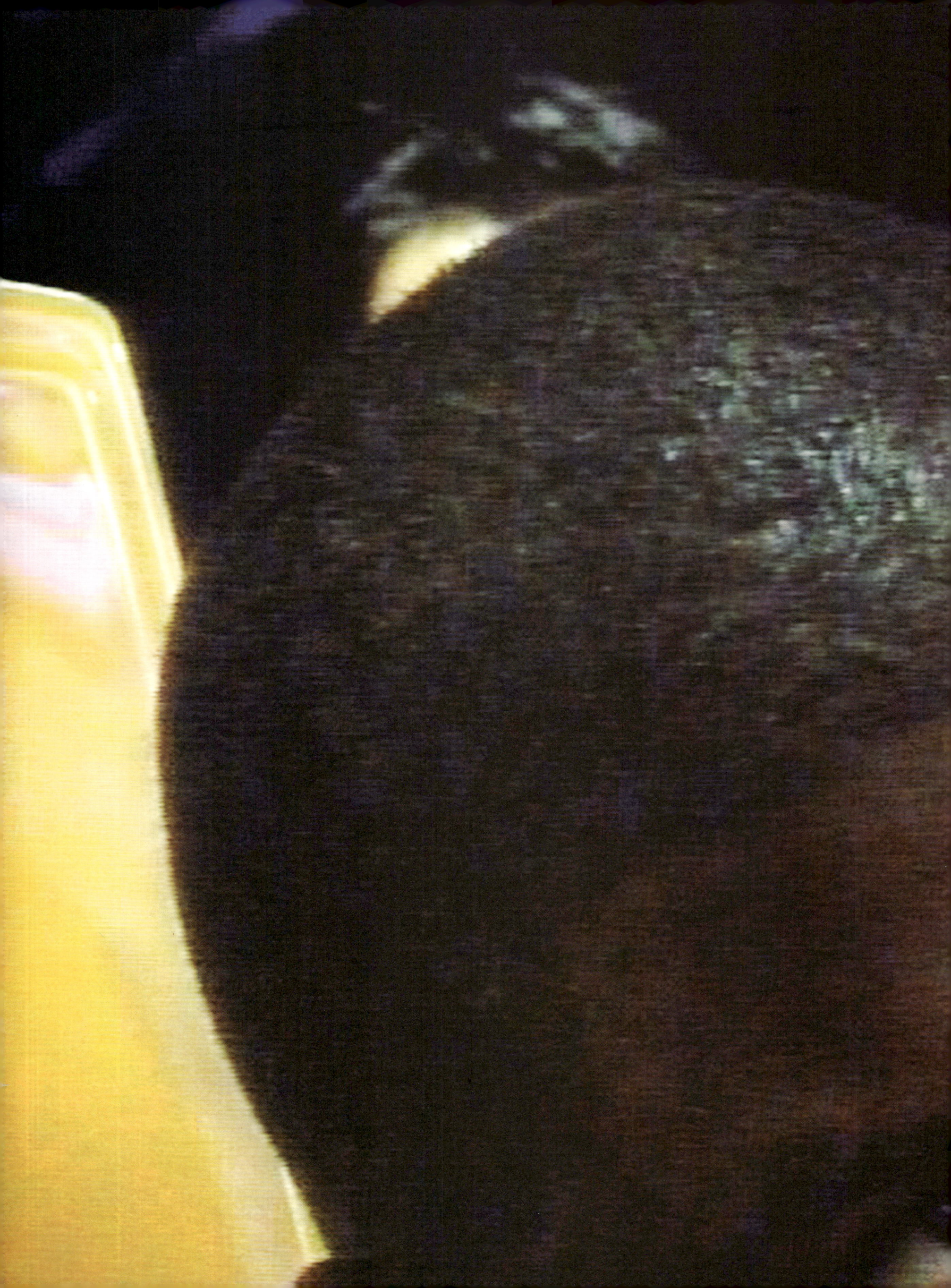

'…That was too close…'

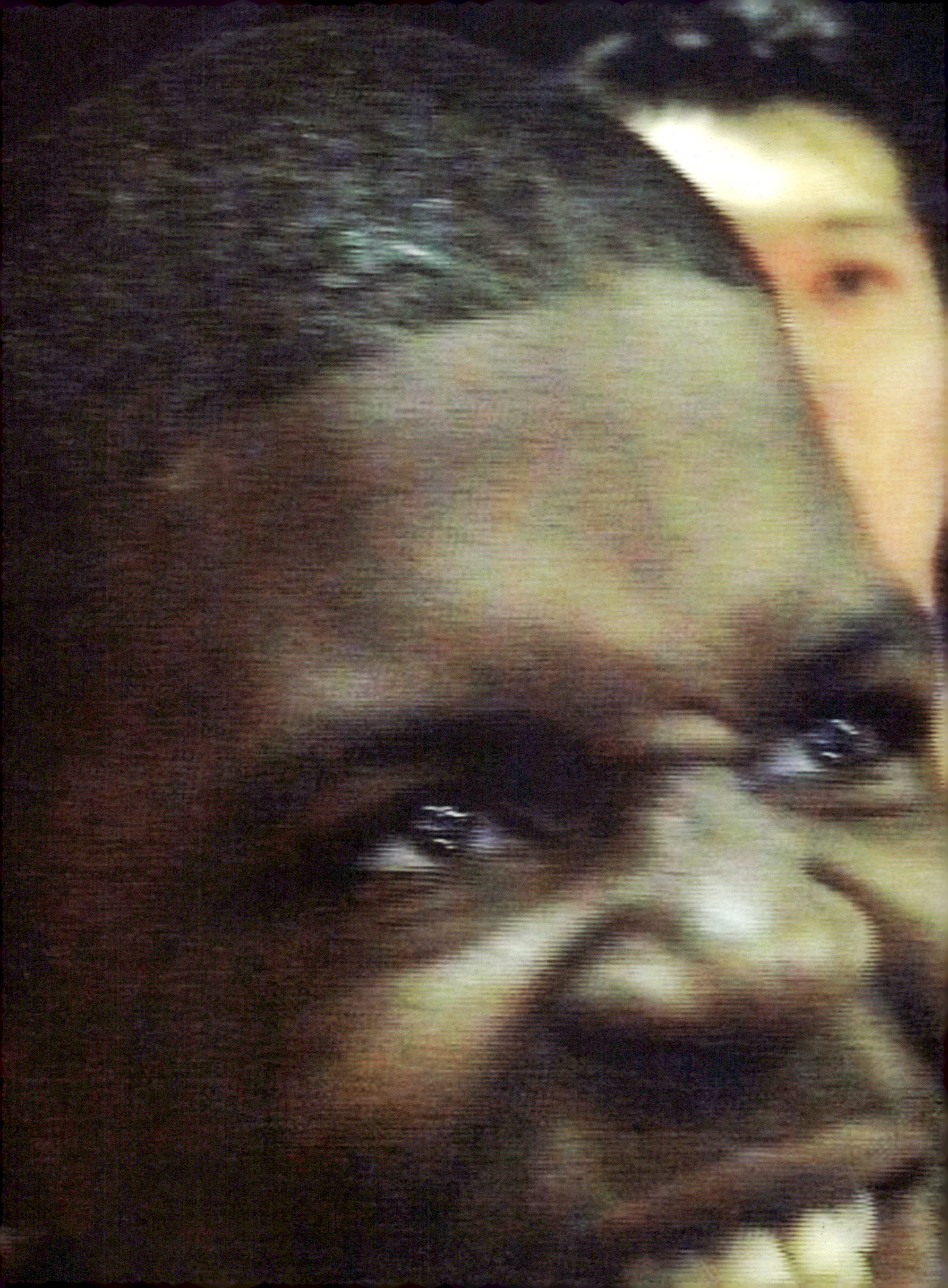

'...The shield is down...'

# Works

Going Down, 1999

Two-monitor DVD installation
32 seconds, looped
Edition of 3 with A/P

Photographs with song-sheets
30.5 cms x 40.6 cms framed
Edition of 5

X, 2000

DVD installation
8 minutes 3 seconds, looped
Edition of 5 with A/P

Talent Show, 2000

Two-monitor DVD installation
2 minutes 44 seconds, looped
Edition of 5 with A/P

Photographs
32 cms x 42 cms framed
Edition of 5

Out of Time, 2001

DVD projection
3 minutes 7 seconds, looped
Edition of 3 with A/P

Photograph
57 cms x 140 cms framed
Key
36 cms x 67.5 cms framed
Edition of 3

This Sporting Life, 2002

Two-monitor DVD installation
4 minutes 41 seconds, looped
Edition of 5 with A/P

The Artist would like to thank

Neil Angle, Debbie Bragg at Every Night Images, Tim Burgess at Barking Mad Productions, Crystal Palace Football Club, East Ham Workingmen's Club, Granada Television, Steve Harper, Ilford Workingmen's Club, Kathy Kenny at Art on Film, Dave Lanning, Optex, London Post, Darren Southee, Lorna Starnes, The Outside Boots Brigade, Keith Tenniswood, Sid Waddell, Nick Wand, Andrew Weatherall, Michael Wray

Anthony Wilkinson, Amanda Knight-Adams and Stuart Taylor at Anthony Wilkinson Gallery, Steven Bode, Caroline Smith and Mike Jones at Film and Video Umbrella, Anne McNeill and staff at Impressions Gallery, York, Paul Bayley and staff at Cornerhouse, Manchester, Sally O'Reilly and Richard Bonner-Morgan

...and a very special thanks to Jim Chynoweth and Emma Henry

# Julie Henry

1959      Born, Cambridge
1993-98  BA Critical Fine Art Practice, Central St Martin's School of Art and Design, London
1992-93  Foundation, Mornington Centre, London

## Solo Exhibitions

2003      Anthony Wilkinson Gallery, London
           BCA Gallery, Bedford
2002      Impressions Gallery, York
2000      Anthony Wilkinson Gallery, London

## Group Exhibitions

2003      Intervention, John Hansard Gallery, Southampton
           Strangers, International Centre of Photography Triennial, New York (Anri Sala, Francis Alys, Shirin Neshat, Philip-Lorca diCorcia, Renee Green, Chein-Chi Chang)
           Somewhere better than this place, Contemporary Arts Center, Cincinnati
2002      Diskourski, Galeria-Arsenal, Poland
           Spectator Sport, (Roderick Buchanan, Julie Henry, Tracey Moffatt, Ravi Deepres and Mark Lewis) Cornerhouse, Manchester
2001      Going Down, Dynamo Kiev, curated by ICA Ukraine
           Sense of Wonder, curated by Harten & Mascher, Herzliya Museum of Art, Israel
           Predator, KX auf Kampnagel, Hamburg, Germany
           Tirana Biennale, Tirana National Gallery, selected by Francesco Bonami
           Sport in der zeitgenossischen Kunst, Kunsthalle Nurnberg, Germany
           Record Collection, VTO Gallery, London
           The Fantastic Recurrence of Certain Situations: Recent British Art and Photography, Sala de Exposiciones del Canal de Isabel II, Madrid, curated by Kate Bush
2000      Rutger Hauer, Perry Motors, London
           Going Down, Oldham Museum and Gallery
1999      Going Down, Edinburgh City Gallery
           New Contemporaries 99, South London Gallery
           New Contemporaries 99, Exchange Flags, Liverpool
1998      World Cup 98, The Final, London Printworks Trust
           Volcano Festival, The Oval House, London
           Going Down, Croydon Clocktower
           My Eyes, My Eyes, Milch Gallery, London and The Silo, Greenwich
1997      Arts Alive Festival, Dorking
           Zone Multi-Media Festival, Maidstone
           Six British Artists, Ars Locus Gallery, Tokyo

Julie Henry
Published by Film and Video Umbrella
Edited by Steven Bode
Editorial assistance by Nina Ernst
Designed by Richard Bonner-Morgan
Printed by Trichrom Limited

Photography by Debbie Bragg and the artist
Installation photographs by Bevis Bowden
Cover and inside front cover from 'Talent Show'
Inside back cover from 'This Sporting Life'

Published to accompany the Film and Video Umbrella touring exhibition, 'This Sporting Life', commissioned in association with Cornerhouse, Manchester and Impressions Gallery, York

Publication supported by the National Touring Programme of the Arts Council of England. With additional support from Anthony Wilkinson Gallery

Printed in an edition of 1,000 copies

© 2003, Film and Video Umbrella, the artist and the authors

ISBN 1904270026

film and video umbrella